World's Scariest Places

Creepy UFO Sites

Alix Wood

Gareth Stevens Publishing

Please visit our website, **www.garethstevens.com**. For a free color catalog of all our high-quality books, call toll free 1-800-542-2595 or fax 1-877-542-2596.

Cataloging-in-Publication Data

Names: Wood, Alix.
Title: Creepy UFO sites / Alix Wood.
Description: New York : Gareth Stevens Publishing, 2020.
| Series: World's scariest places | Includes glossary and index.
Identifiers: ISBN 9781538242575 (pbk.) | ISBN 9781538242018 (library bound) | ISBN 9781538242582 (6 pack)
Subjects: LCSH: Unidentified flying objects--Juvenile literature.
| Human-alien encounters--Juvenile literature.
Classification: LCC TL789.2W64 2020 | DDC 001.942--dc23

First Edition

Published in 2020 by
Gareth Stevens Publishing
111 East 14th Street, Suite 349
New York, NY 10003

Produced for Gareth Stevens by Alix Wood Books
Designed by Alix Wood
Editor: Eloise Macgregor

Photo credits:
Cover, 1, 3, 4, 5, 6, 7, 8, 10, 12 top, 13, 14-15, 16-17, 21, 23 inset, 24, 27 foreground, 28, 29 bottom © Adobe Stock Images; 11 © Henry Parker; 15 top © USAF; 17 inset © Manuela Bilu; 18 inset © Matthew Freeman/US Navy; 18 bottom © Rob Tabor/US Navy; 19, 22 © Alix Wood/Adobe Stock Images; 23 bottom © J. Cornelius; 24 background © Davis Cohen; 25 top © Roswell Daily Record; 25 middle and bottom © Fort Worth Star-Telegram Photograph Collection; 26 © Graham Maclachlan; 29 top © National Archives and Records Administration; all other images are in the public domain

Printed in the United States of America

CPSIA compliance information: Batch #CS19GS. For further information contact Gareth Stevens, New York, New York at 1-800-542-2595.

Contents

People studying space have found several other planets that could support life. If intelligent **aliens** do exist, they may well have paid us a visit at some time! If they did, they would probably have visited in a UFO. Short for "unidentified flying object," UFOs are believed to have been spotted in the sky all over the world. Do you believe aliens from outer space are visiting us?

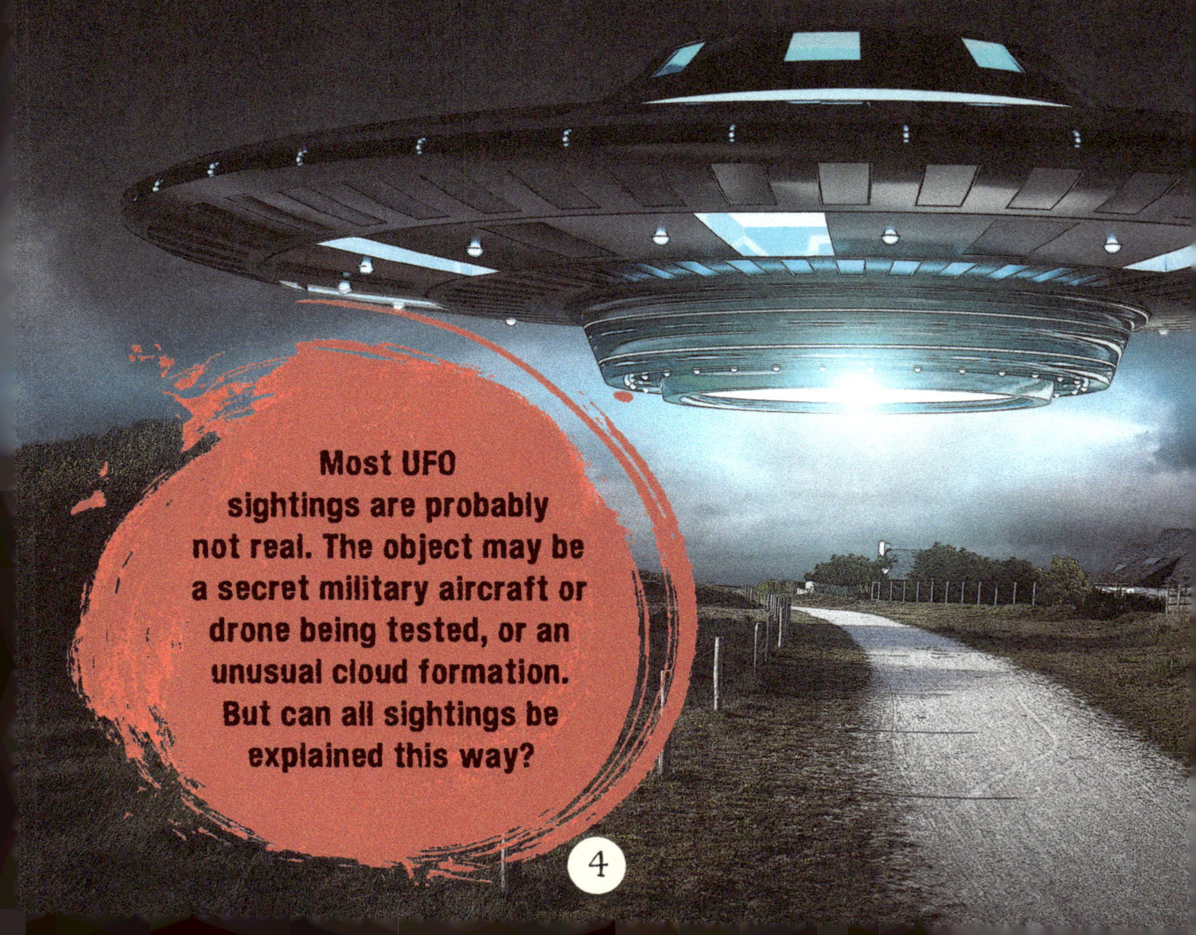

Most UFO sightings are probably not real. The object may be a secret military aircraft or drone being tested, or an unusual cloud formation. But can all sightings be explained this way?

Many governments believe UFOs may exist. These telescopes at the University of California are used by an organization known as SETI (the Search for **Extraterrestrial** Intelligence). They hunt for any sign of communication from other planets in the universe.

2013, Chelyabinsk, Russia. A giant **meteor** on a collision course with Earth mysteriously exploded moments before it hit the city. At the point it exploded, people saw what looked like a UFO! Are aliens protecting our planet? Some people think so!

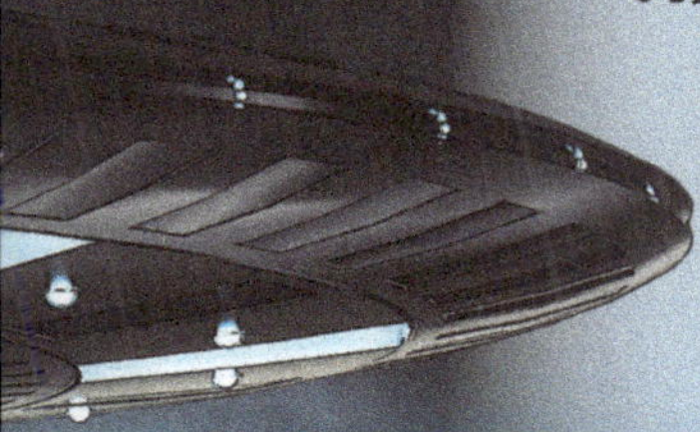

Kansas City, Kansas

Airline pilot Andrew Danzinger took off from Kansas City one fine spring evening in 1989. Once in the air, Danzinger and his captain both saw a strange, white, disc-shaped object out of the right cockpit window. The white disc wasn't the moon, as the pilots could still see that out of the other window. They checked the ground in case it was a searchlight, but there were none.

Pilots spend many hours flying up above the clouds. Many of them say they have seen unusual objects while in the air that they cannot explain.

As the pilots came in to land, they looked away. When they looked back, the disc had become a giant red ball! It went behind a cloud, and hundreds of flashing lights appeared. The cloud then tore apart. The lights vanished. Spooked, the men checked with air traffic control, who said there were no other flights near them. Danzinger told the National UFO Reporting Center. They said other pilots had reported a similar experience, but they had no idea what it was!

Air traffic controllers track all aircraft in their area. They make sure everyone is safe in the sky and organize flights as they take off and land. Sometimes, they spot flying objects they can't explain, too.

RAF Oldenburg, Germany

A UFO sighting by an RAF pilot once convinced a UK government minister that aliens had visited Earth's **airspace**. In July 1952, Flight Sergeant Roland Hughes was flying his de Havilland Vampire over West Germany when he saw something that made him radio his base at once.

A gleaming silver disc had flown beside his aircraft, and then sped away. Ground **radar** recorded the mysterious object speeding faster than any known aircraft!

An artist's impression of the metallic disc

Hughes was sent by his superiors to see the Aviation Minister, Duncan Sandys, to report on what he had seen. Sandys was convinced by Hughes's story, particularly as several U.S. airmen had recently had similar experiences. In his report, Sandys wrote that there was "ample evidence of some unfamiliar and unexplained **phenomenon**."

After his UFO experience, Hughes was known to his colleagues as "Saucer Sam!" His Vampire had a UFO painted on it with his new name underneath!

"SAUCER SAM" STANDING NEXT TO HIS VAMPIRE

Elmwood, Wisconsin

In 1976, police officer George Wheeler was on an evening patrol. He saw what he thought was a fire up on Tuttle Hill. He radioed the incident in and drove his squad car up to investigate. He soon got a clear view of the area, and to his surprise he saw a silver, glowing object hovering over the hill.

The Elmwood UFO was huge, silver, and had a bright orange light coming from a domed roof. As it rose into the air, a blue ray shot from the bottom of the spaceship!

A ray from the UFO hit Wheeler's squad car. His police radio and vehicle lights went dead. When local farmer David Moots found Wheeler's squad car in the middle of the road, Wheeler was unconscious. When Wheeler woke up, he told Moots he had been hit by a UFO! Other local people saw the orange glow that night. Nearby dogs would not stop barking, and some TVs and radios suddenly stopped working.

Elmwood holds a UFO festival every year, but it is not the only town in Wisconsin that claims to be visited by aliens. Belleville and Dundee also claim to be UFO capitals. There is so much UFO activity in the state that a welder in Poland, Wisconsin, built this UFO landing port!

Petrozavodsk, Russia

In September 1977, around 4 a.m. in the skies above the Russian city of Petrozavodsk, many people saw what they described as a large, shining jellyfish! Similar sightings were also reported at Helsinki in Finland, and Vladivostok right on the other side of Russia. At first, onlookers saw a bright, fiery ball in the sky that spiraled closer. The ball then stopped, hovering for around six minutes, making a howling noise!

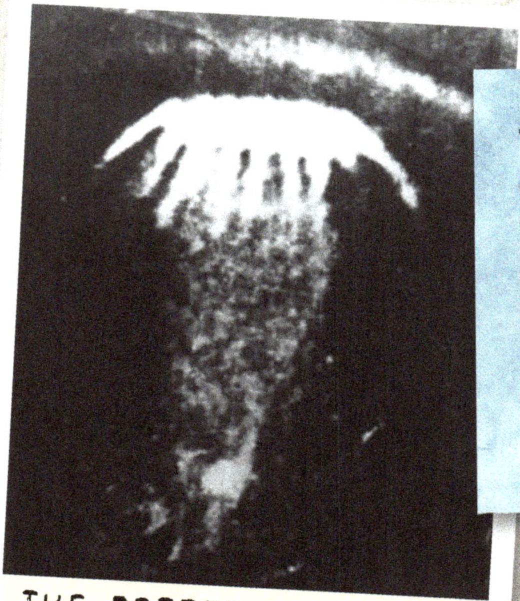

THE PETROZAVODSK UFO

This photograph taken of the strange "jellyfish" shows the disc-shaped object, with its showering beams of light. People described the beams as being beautiful colors, and looking like heavy rain.

The pulsing ball of fire suddenly went quiet. Two beams of light shot out of the bottom of the object and hundreds of rays of light showered down, making it appear like a jellyfish. The rays created onion-size holes in some road surfaces and glass windows! People started to panic. The object headed to nearby Lake Onega. It burned a hole in clouds over the lake and disappeared, surrounded by semicircles of pink light!

What was it that was witnessed by so many people? Experts studying the incident think it was a rocket. A spy satellite was launched from a nearby secret space station at around the same time.

Washington, D.C.

Just before midnight, July 19, 1952. Washington National Airport air traffic controller Edward Nugent noticed seven unknown objects moving in an unusual manner on his radar. His boss checked the radar for faults. It was working fine.

They contacted nearby National Airport. Their radar had also noticed unusual activity and their controllers had seen a hovering bright light that suddenly sped away. When UFOs were spotted above the White House and Capitol Building, controllers quickly radioed Andrews Air Force Base!

Two Air Force F-94 jets raced to the scene. Each time the jets reached the last radar location, the objects would disappear! The following Saturday, a pilot and stewardess on a flight into Washington saw strange lights above them. Airport radar showed more UFOs, sometimes traveling at incredible speeds! Two F-94s gave chase but could not catch the objects.

Experts decided the radar **blips** were caused by a layer of warm air trapping cooler air beneath. Radar signals can bounce off this layer, making it appear as if there is an object in the sky. But the controllers still believed what they saw could not be explained this way.

Hoia Baciu Forest, Romania

This spooky forest in Romania is home to several sightings of both UFOs and ghosts! People visiting the forest sometimes experience illness, anxiety, rashes, and even burns to their skin. Ghostly faces have been known to appear in photographs taken in the forest. Then, in the 1960s, the forest was said to be visited by a UFO!

This photograph of a UFO over the Hoia Baciu Forest was one of four taken by Emil Barnea in 1968. He, his girlfriend, and two friends stopped to eat lunch in a clearing in the forest. His girlfriend spotted a strange object in the sky and called him over. Emil grabbed his camera from his bag and took photos.

Experts who examined his photos say they show no obvious signs of being fake. They estimate the UFO was around 98 feet (30 m) across and made of metal.

Much of the forest's strange activity takes place in this clearing. Nothing ever grows there. Mysterious floating lights and ghostly figures have been seen. Some think the clearing may even be a pathway to another universe!

Strange, misshapen trees add to the forest's spooky atmosphere. Several of the trees have oddly charred stumps or branches.

Pacific Ocean, Near San Diego

Between November 10 and November 16, 2004, a navy crew 100 miles (160 km) off the coast of San Diego noticed some strange activity on their radar. Objects could be seen dropping at great speed from high in the sky to hover just above the water. Then the objects sped away. USS *Nimitz* sent two of its FA-18F Super Hornets to investigate.

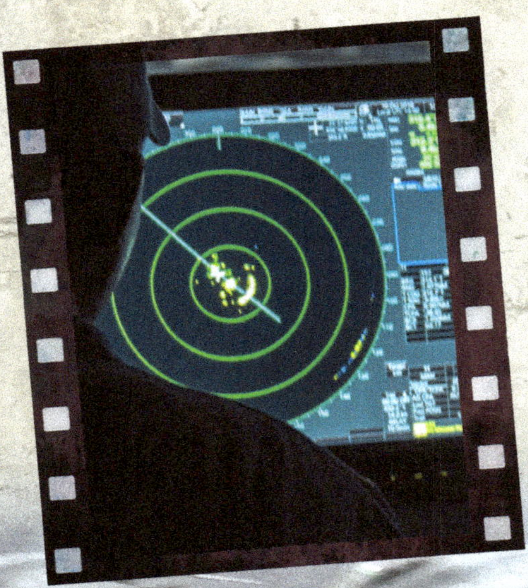

A SUPER HORNET TAKES OFF

When the pilots reached the location, they found an area of churning water. An object was hovering above the ocean. The object then sped away at three times the **speed of sound**, and twice as fast as the fighter jets!

Nearby USS *Princeton* also picked up the unidentified craft on its radar. It had flown to exactly where the Hornets had been before being sent to intercept! Another FA-18 was scrambled, and found more disturbed water on the ocean surface

The pilots described the object as looking like a tic tac candy! It had no wings or windows, and no exhaust fumes.

Erasmuskloof, South Africa

In a suburb of Pretoria, South Africa, on an early August morning in 1996, a strange glowing disc appeared in the sky. Police Sergeant Johann Becker spotted the object. It had a red triangular light, and shining green tentacles! When Becker called for backup, he was laughed at. But as more people called in to report it, officers, police dogs, and a helicopter were sent!

Helicopter pilot Colonel Fred Vijoen could not keep up with the speed the disc was traveling. He had to give up the chase when the UFO shot upward and he worried he would run out of fuel.

There were plenty of witnesses to this UFO sighting! Around 200 police officers were sent to investigate. They watched the object flying above them for 90 minutes. Sergeant Nico Stander filmed a video of the object, which he gave to investigators. They described the film as showing the disc moving through the sky like a falling leaf. Helicopter pilot Fred Vijoen was convinced what he had seen was not an aircraft. His four passengers on board agreed with him.

Radar operators in Johannesburg also saw something unusual on their screens that morning. The control tower at Waterkloof Air Force Base said their radar showed "clutter" in the area in which the disc was flying.

Aurora, Texas

One of the first ever UFO sightings happened in Aurora, Texas, back in April 17, 1897! A cigar-shaped craft was seen flying over the town and crashed into a windmill on property owned by Judge Proctor. The UFO then burst into flames and scattered **debris** over nearby land. The remains of an alien creature is said to have been found in the wreckage.

Local resident S.E. Haydon sent a report to the local paper.

The Dallas Morning News

ALIEN CRASHES IN AURORA!

About 6 o'clock this morning the early risers of Aurora were astonished at the sudden appearance of the airship which has been sailing around the country. It was traveling due north and much nearer the earth than before. Evidently some of the machinery was out of order,

The pilot of the ship is supposed to have been the only one aboard and, while his remains were badly disfigured, enough of the original has been picked up to show that he was not an inhabitant of this world.

Mr. T. J. Weems, the United States signal service officer at this place and an authority on astronomy, gives it as

The alien was said to have been given a Christian burial in an unmarked grave in the local cemetery. Some of the wreckage was reportedly buried with the alien. A grave marker was later made to mark the site, but it was stolen in 1972. A replacement marker was also removed in 2012.

Some wreckage is thought to have been thrown down Proctor's well. When new owner Brawley Oates cleared the well, he got bad arthritis. Oates blamed the alien metal for his illness, and sealed up the well.

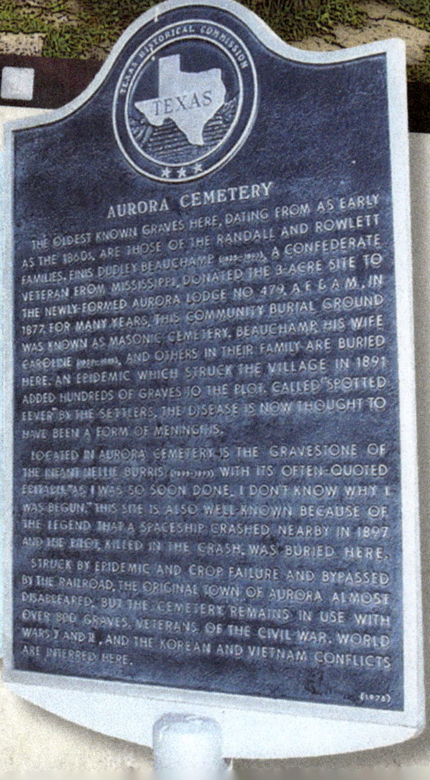

This sign in the Aurora cemetery reads "a spaceship crashed nearby in 1897 and the pilot, killed in the crash, was buried here." Is it true? Some think the story was a hoax. Haydon may have written the news article to try to keep the town alive after hundreds had died from a terrible disease and its cotton crop had failed.

Roswell, New Mexico

In the summer of 1947, a strange flying disc crashed in the desert near the town of Roswell. Eyewitnesses had seen a blazing object in the sky shortly before the impact. Debris scattered at the crash site looked very unusual. Rumors began to spread that the mysterious aircraft was a UFO!

Alien bodies were said to have been recovered by the military from the Roswell crash site.

Roswell Daily Record

RECORD PHONES
Business Office 2288
News Department 2287

RAAF Captures Flying Saucer On Ranch in Roswell Region

House Passes ax Slash by rge Margin

Security Council Paves Way to Talks On Arms Reductions

No Details of Flying Disk Are Revealed

Roswell Hardware Man and Wife Report Disk Seen

Ex-King Carol Weds Mme. Lupescu

Miners and Operators Sign Highest Wage Pact in History

American League

Roswell Army Air Field (RAAF) specialists investigated the crash site. The army information officer then told the local paper that the aircraft was a UFO (right).

The day after the accident, the military said the UFO was a weather balloon. People who had seen the debris didn't believe this. Was the military covering up what they found?

a weather balloon

Doctors were rumored to have examined aliens with skinny arms and huge, bald heads! A faked film of an alien **autopsy** was released. In the 1990s, the military finally said the crash had been a top-secret nuclear test **surveillance** balloon! What do you think is true?

the crash debris

Llandrillo, Wales

On January 23, 1974, people in the Welsh village of Llandrillo noticed strange, bright lights streaking across the night sky. Later that night, their houses were rocked by an explosion, followed by a terrifying rumble. People saw what looked like fire on the nearby mountain. Police and military teams rushed to the site and searched the area. Rumors spread that they had found wreckage and bodies from a UFO. The event jokingly became known as "Roswelsh" after the similar incident in Roswell, New Mexico.

The mountains near Llandrillo were sealed off by the search teams. Local people became suspicious that something out of this world had crashed there.

That night, police telephoned a local nurse and asked her to help at a plane crash near Llandrillo. As she drove up the mountainside she saw a large, circular object on the ground. It was glowing orange! It didn't look like an aircraft, and it didn't look as if it had crashed. It looked just like a UFO! The nurse explained to the search teams why she was there, but they quickly rushed her off the mountain! Had the search teams found something top secret there?

Recently released military documents suggest the event was caused by a meteor, followed by an earthquake. What do you think?

Bermuda Triangle, Atlantic Ocean

A triangular-shaped area of the Atlantic Ocean is the center of a strange mystery. An unusual number of aircraft and ships have disappeared there.

Many pilots and sailors dislike crossing this area of ocean. Compasses will often become faulty. Stories are told of boats and aircraft being swallowed by a swirling **vortex**.

Some believe the strange events may be caused by aliens! Unexplained glowing orbs and halos have been seen in the sky over the Bermuda Triangle.

On December 5, 1945, an entire squadron of planes went missing in the Bermuda Triangle. Flight 19's five torpedo bombers flew east from Fort Lauderdale, Florida, on a training mission. Not one of them returned. A search and rescue aircraft was sent to hunt for them. It also disappeared with 13 men on board! What happened? Experts believe they may have all simply run out of fuel!

Why does this area of the Atlantic swallow up ships and aircraft? It may be due to difficult weather conditions, or it could be pilots and captains making mistakes. Explorer Darrell Miklos believes a vast object he found on the seabed could be a UFO that crashed to Earth thousands of years ago. Could its discovery suggest aliens have been behind the disappearances at sea?

Glossary

airspace the air available to aircraft to fly in

aliens beings that come from another world

arthritis inflammation of the joints

autopsy an examination of a dead body

blips spots on a screen

debris the remains of something broken down or destroyed

drones aircraft or ships without a pilot, controlled by radio signals

extraterrestrial coming from outside Earth or its atmosphere

hoax something false passed off or accepted as genuine

meteor a small piece of matter that falls from space with great speed, producing a bright light as it enters Earth's atmosphere

phenomenon a rare or important fact or event

radar a device that sends out radio waves to detect objects by the reflection of the radio waves

speed of sound the speed that sound travels through the air: one mile in 4.7 seconds (1 km in 2.9 seconds)

surveillance close watch

vortex a mass of whirling fluid forming a cavity in the center toward which things are drawn

Further Information

Borgert-Spaniol, Megan. *UFOs: Are Alien Aircraft Overhead? (Science Fact or Science Fiction?)*. North Mankato, MN: Checkerboard Library, 2018.

Polydoros, Lori. *Top 10 UFO and Alien Mysteries*. Mankato, MN: Capstone Press, 2015.

Website

CBC Kids page all about UFOs
https://www.cbc.ca/kidscbc2/the-feed/what-exactly-are-ufos

Publisher's note to educators and parents:
Our editors have carefully reviewed these websites to ensure that they are suitable for students. Many websites change frequently, however, and we cannot guarantee that a site's future contents will continue to meet our high standards of quality and educational value. Be advised that students should be closely supervised whenever they access the Internet.

Index